The Dissection of a Tiger

THE DISSECTION OF A TIGER

poetry by tyler walter

QUERENCIA PRESS

© Copyright 2023
tyler walter

ISBN 978 1 959118 26 8

www.querenciapress.com

First Published in 2023

Querencia Press, LLC
Chicago IL

Printed & Bound in the United States of America

CONTENTS

he holds me in his arms like a lover, his open mouth against my neck.

the dream

sometimes the tiger could be looking through you
rather than at you. sometimes the tiger could be
aiming for the spot behind you rather than your neck.
occasionally you think the tiger is a friend. not a thing
to be feared but something that could be loved. it
makes you stop. that look in his eyes that says he's
scared too. he's thinking the same. you're not just prey
you're something that could be loved. what the tiger wants
is not always obvious. but his teeth are always sharp
and you always end up bleeding.

is the gate secure is the hedge high enough can you run fast is the door locked are your shoes tied can it jump here's the test here it goes and jump and run this is it this is the end is it is it is it where do you go from here do you know this place do you know these streets why isn't anyone helping why isn't anyone helping who are you what do you want please help the blood is hot the sun is hot the teeth are glinting here they come here they come here they—

tiger in love

the first night was the hardest
i knew you were coming i waited
breathed in the desert air shifted
my weight from one foot to another
i knew you were coming something
was different changed there was a
sweet taste in my mouth a promise
for something more to come inhale
exhale get ready to run get ready
i knew you were coming and i
couldn't wait i could hear my own
heartbeat as if outside myself
and i felt it jump when you arrived
it had been your fear i could taste
and it only became stronger i
couldn't help myself i swear
all this excitement got to me

i'm never usually like this
the anticipation
was too much oh god i thought
you loved me i thought
you were just as excited
and that's why you were
screaming
and then i realised
the blood my teeth
your heart in my hands
it only made me want you more.

i could miss him if he'd let me go

i think at first i was scared
i think i must have been scared
i never make eye contact first
my mother once called me rude
when i didn't look at her
there are too many ways
to say this and not enough
time
i think at first i was scared
that he'd see right through me
that he'd see what i was
really scared of
i blushed i think too when i met him
pink in the desert sunlight or
pink under grocery store lights
it's hard to know when
the first time was

i blushed and he thought
i was lovely he said that
he would just lovelovelove
to get his claws into me
he said it while smiling
or at least i thought that
seeing his teeth meant
that he was smiling
when i move his claws
draw blood
i don't think he means it
i don't think he knows
he's an animal
running on instinct.

the moon an eye

the first night was the easiest
sleep was never easy but that night
it fell quickly the moon was high
i knew the desert like a second home
knew each grain of sand already
two boys in the distance i knew
their names their hopes what they
each thought the outcome would be
i knew you tiger already i knew you
before i ever met you there before
you broke my flesh into pieces
tiger you were waiting for me
i was glad that there was someone
who would wait for me glad that
you and i were linked that i
was not alone in the world

the moment we made eye contact

was the moment we fell

and knew our fates too

i was destined to run

you were destined to capture

kill eat survive

the first night was the easiest

i ran to that grocery store

we both knew it like we know

each other tiger that night

was the only night that i considered

that there could be a different ending

i wondered about an ending full

of love and life but tiger you know

that our ending has love in it

our ending has life in it even if its
not mine our ending happens
over and over each night is like
the first it hasn't gotten harder
to sleep again tiger listen the moon
is high tonight tiger i'll see
you tonight and tomorrow
and the night after that too.

say something

i'm nowhere near ur heart baby
baby listen if i wanted u dead u would be
don't worry these claws won't reach
baby listen ur doing okay now ur doing okay
ur alive and i'm alive and we're together baby
they don't go too deep i'll miss ur heart by miles i swear
i just want to feel how warm u are baby how hot
the blood under ur skin is how alive u are baby
because that's the thing isn't it baby ur heart
is beating too fast don't be scared listen baby
i said that if i wanted u dead u would be so don't
make me push my claws any further
i don't think they'll reach ur heart but
do u want to take that chance?

caged

aren't we both stuck here my love?

our own separate cages to pace

lie down my love u can feel the sun

soak it in let it make a home oh god

i think i could fall in love here

i'm sure i could fall in love here with u

forget the fences for a minute

imagine this: we are side by side

looking at the clouds talking about

what life could be like up there

i'll take u with me baby i will i promise

if i get out i'll get u out too and

honey i swear if u hurt me it'll be

worth it i'll thank u because

i'm alive i'm alive i'm alive and i'm bleeding

ur alive ur alive ur alive and i'm bleeding

out on the linoleum oh god i think

i'd fall in love further if only u could touch me.

tiger's lament

when god made me i think
he just wanted to see how many
exit wounds he could fit onto one body
i hold my breath around u
i think we could work out
if we never look the other in the eye
i'm always looking at what ur hands are holding
always making notes of how u sound walking
on my floor i think god made me for someone else
or maybe he just wanted me to bleed baby
i hear ur laugh from miles away and
it makes me panic i'm not lonely but
i wish god would speak
i'm not trying to change u
but my jaw aches all the goddamn time
and the aching reminds me of u

bring him peace, bring him joy, he is young, he is only a boy

oh god he never meant it i know
he didn't mean it. one day i dream
and he isn't there. oh god i miss him
like an empty grave misses a body.
something has been carved
out of me and not replaced.
something i didn't love or hate
but something that was me and mine
my chest feels like a cave in this dream
one i could crawl into alone one that
fills with water when it rains this cave
echoes and echoes and echoes and echoes
oh god what do i do here without him?

the sun is too much and not enough

i'm overwhelmed and bored of it.

i beg for him to come back to me

back to my body and my dreams.

please. the desert turning into a cave but

oh god i think i could've gotten used to the sun

could u love urself if u were safe

could u really
u know ur lonely
on a pier waiting for the water to move
ur going in circles all the time
is it going to kill u? it has the power to
and maybe there was always something missing
maybe there's always going to be something missing
a sorta heaven like place or
a more tender life
but love is always so close to danger
u've left behind something others can see, something real
doesn't guilt feel like it has its hands inside u
i want u to acknowledge there's more than this
we don't have to survive alone in all the blood
things are starting to collapse
everything is starting to collapse
we are always just a moment away

the comfort that comes with other people

a coin flip

have u made the right choice

how we know what loneliness is like

could u love urself if u were safe

could u love somebody else

for that night

when ur together in the same place

someone might be singing

someone might be listening

tiger loves a cage

baby ur unlike any other
baby ur hot blood is unlike any other
i love u like blood loves a shark
i love u like a light loves a moth
baby i think i'd kill u if u gave me the chance
our love is unlike any other if u
so much as look at me again my heart
might beat through my ribcage into ur hands
i love u like the rain loves a wild rabbit
huddled under leaves and branches i love u
even when u hide even when u don't hide even
when ur begging me to touch u
even when u can see my claws are out and ur
still begging me to touch u
baby just for u i think i could
come here if u want to i won't force it

i love u like a tiger loves a cage

familiar and wonderfully uncomfortable

baby i think my heart's beating through my ribs

come catch it in ur hands. come closer

i often think to myself: this is it. this is it. this is it

bite wound knife wound bullet wound

i'm not going to cry when i leave
you love like a hole in the head
when i start writing poems about you
i think that's when you'll die
you love like a beehive the noises
the colours the working working working
you love like an empty bottle
there was once something there
something to calm you down
i'm not going to cry when i leave
i'm not going to write poems about leaving
i promise there's so much more to us
than the space we grow between us
you love like a puppy scratching at the door
like the wolf howling like the fish gasping
if you cry when i leave please hide your face

i never know what to say never know if
i should touch you or let you get used to
absence
i'm not going to cry when i leave
but god i'll bawl when i get there.

familiarity

nights are like human lives they're all too brief
tiger when i wake i'm still thinking about you
the glint of the desert sun on your teeth
the green of your eyes tiger i hear your voice
everywhere and grocery shopping isn't the same
if my heart isn't being pulled out through my neck
isn't the same if i can't smell my own blood
all this waiting i'm tired of it tired of the daylight
tiger when did i start wanting to see you?
tiger when did i start looking forward to your
hot breath? your claws on my skin?
i swear tiger it feels like love

fragile

ur lying on the grocery store floor in the frozen aisle. ur neck is an open wound. a mess of bone and blood and tendons. i still think i could kiss u. ur all inside out back to front. i'll put it all back where it's supposed to be. stay still. let me touch u. ur blood is seeping into the freezer units and they glow red. baby i think i could stay here like this with u however long. hold my hands and make them warm. i'll hold ur still heart like water cupped in my palms. i love u. do u feel it in the way i'm shaking? i promise i'll keep it safe. i'll pull it out thru the mess of ur neck. still warm and full. i love u. i love u and i don't want ur heart to go to waste. i'll put everything back except this. i'll be careful with it. i'll sink my teeth in.

AND I'M SORRY IF YOU THOUGHT THESE WERE ROMANTIC. I'M SORRY BABY IF YOU THOUGHT THAT EATING YOUR HEART MEANT I LOVED YOU. I'M JUST LOOKING FOR SOMEONE TO FEED ME I'VE BEEN SO HUNGRY HUNGRY HUNGRY I'M SO HUNGRY HUNGRY HUNGRY ALL THE DAMN TIME. DID YOU NOT THINK I KNEW WHAT WOULD HAPPEN? DID YOU NOT THINK THAT I WANTED THIS TO HAPPEN? ARE YOU DUMB OR BLINDED BY LOVE? BABY I'M SORRY BUT EVEN ANIMALS HAVE TO EAT. I TAKE WHAT I CAN GET I SAW YOUR FLESH AND I WAS HOOKED BABY CAN YOU BLAME ME? I'LL MAKE IT QUICK IF ONLY YOU'D JUST STAND STILL. IF ONLY YOU'D JUST LET ME.

jung

in this dream i am neither the tiger nor myself. here i am the desert and the sky. i am each grain of sand that burns under the sun. i am the sunlight, orange and relentless. i am the two boys playing, i am each of their thoughts, i am all four of their hands, the teeth in their smiles. i am the grocery store windows, the shelves inside, the empty freezer units. i am glowing white and red. i am the dust in the air, the white noise of a tannoy. i am concrete, plastic, glass. i am hot and cold and colder still. i am the fence as it is jumped over. i am the blood on the floor, on clothing, on fur.

his heart's not in it but then again neither's mine

tiger seems distracted today clumsy
tripping over his own paws his eyes
don't focus on me his claws don't
extend the full way i know they can
his jaw doesn't have the same strength
and he had to try a few times to jump
over the fence. tiger seems distracted
or sad almost. his heart's not in it so
when he pounces and when his breath
is hot on my skin and when his teeth
are holding my neck i move my hands
towards his face i hold his cheeks in
my palms and stroke the fur there

gently gently tiger it's okay to not be
with it all the time. you can have your
off days your sad days tiger it's okay
you can rest. look tiger i'll rip
my own throat out for you. rip
my heart out through my neck and bleed
and bleed and bleed i can do that for you
tiger. you can be distracted. you can rest.

dissection

are you sleep deprived

does the caged tiger make you sad

how fast can you run

what does blood smell like

aren't you hungry

would you let the tiger free

can you jump high

have you been sleeping well

aren't you hungry

do you have nightmares too

what do you want to eat

does blood stain fur

would you cage yourself to escape the tiger

do you wake shaking

do you think the tiger is smiling

why is it so dark here

aren't you so so hungry

where is the lightswitch

does metal smell like blood or—

do you slip on linoleum floors

are you tired

does it hurt

does it really hurt

are you going to sleep?

everything all at once (or what actually happened)

here's the dream:
the desert. hot sand
concrete and a fence
a jungle lies between that
and another fence
wire criss-crossed
then a grocery store
where two boys dressed in white
play outside by the windows
i think they might break—
and then there's a tiger
between the two fences
sunk into the green between them
claws through the fence
he snarls growls roars

i've always heard that
a tiger's roar is more powerful
than a lion's and his vibrates
the concrete under my feet
my heart beats in my ears
i worry for the two boys
who haven't noticed the tiger
but he's focused on me he jumps
over the fence toward me
and i run
and run and run and run and run
desert and buildings made of mud
and straw and then the grocery store
bright white modern and shining
the boys have disappeared or have
been eaten i run into the store
without looking behind

in the freezer aisle the lights

are more blinding than usual

the units glow empty

and then the tiger is there

i know by the sound

of his breath

he's behind me

and i've stopped running

i turn

and something happens:

i fall in love

                    his teeth close around my throat

i kiss his cheeks, his forehead

                    he tears the tendons from my neck

i tell him i don't blame him

                    he puts his claws into my chest

i hold him gently as we lie together

                    he rips my heart out, whole and bloody

i offer him my body

                    i offer him my body

notes

the dream
'what the tiger wants / is not always obvious' is paraphrased from Kevin Young's poem 'Replicas' in which they write 'what the ghost wants // is not always / obvious'.

tiger's lament
inspired by Ocean Vuong's title to his poetry book 'Night Sky with Exit Wounds'.

bring him peace, bring him joy, he is young, he is only a boy
the title comes from a line in the song 'Bring Him Home' in the musical Les Miserables.

could u love urself if u were safe
this poem is a found poem using lines from an almost-essay I wrote for a friend explaining my love for Richard Siken's poem 'You Are Jeff'.

familiarity
the first line 'nights are like human lives they're all too brief' is a translated quote from the anime Samurai Champloo.

jung

named for the psychologist who posited that we are everything in our own dreams and so should consider this when analysing their meaning.

everything all at once (or what actually happened)

this is a recount as far as I can remember of the actual dream from which these poems came from. I remember all of it vividly, except for the end.

Ingram Content Group UK Ltd.
Milton Keynes UK
UKHW050629190623
423681UK00010B/498